Waterways TO THE Great Lakes

Great Lakes of North America

Harry Beckett

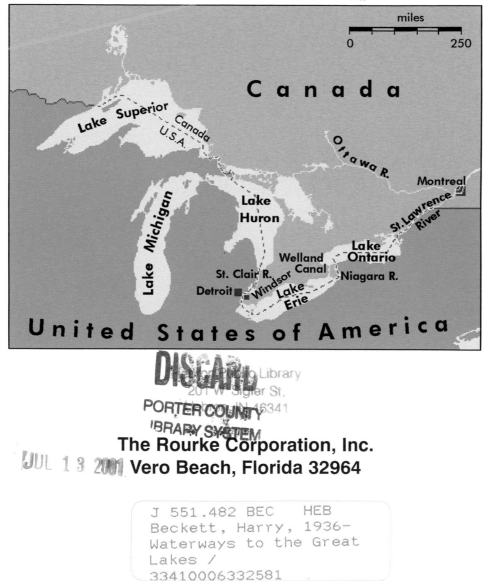

The Rourke Corporation, Inc.
Vero Beach, Florida 32964

PHOTO CREDITS:
Photographs by kind permission of: Rapid Magazine, Scott McGregor; Michigan Sea Grant; National Archives of Canada; Michigan Division of Tourism; Geovisuals, Waterloo, Ont.; Wasaga Beach Provincial Park; Maps by David J. Knox

CREATIVE SERVICES:
East Coast Studios, Merritt Island, Florida

EDITORIAL SERVICES:
Susan Albury

Library of Congress Cataloging-in-Publication Data

Beckett, Harry, 1936-
   Waterways to the Great Lakes / by Harry Beckett.
      p. cm. — (Great Lakes of North America)
   Includes bibliographical references and index.
   Summary: Describes the history, climate, wildlife, and different bodies of water of the Saint Lawrence-Great Lake Waterway.
      ISBN 0-86593-529-7
   1. Saint Lawrence River Juvenile literature. [1. Saint Lawrence River 2. Great Lakes.] I. Title. II. Series: Beckett, Harry, 1936- Great Lakes of North America.
F1050.B43 1999
551.48'2'0977—DC21
                                                                    99-23310
                                                                         CIP

Printed in the USA

TABLE OF CONTENTS

HOW THE LAKES WERE FORMED

The rocks of the lake beds were formed by great volcanic activity about 3 billion years ago. The volcanic rock was folded and formed into high mountains. Over many millions of years, these were **eroded** (eh RODE id) until they became the rolling hills and low mountains of today's **Canadian Shield** (kuh NAY dee un SHE(u)LD). Also called the Laurentian Highlands, this area covers Quebec and Ontario provinces in Canada and parts of Minnesota, Wisconsin, Michigan, and New York in the United States.

Quebec City with the St. Lawrence River in the foreground

Later, seas flooded the land for a period of time, covering it with silt and sand that eventually turned into a layer of limestone and shale over the volcanic rock.

The lakes were formed when glaciers, up to 6,500 feet (2,000 meters) thick, moved southward and scraped away the surface rocks. The ice deepened and widened the river valleys to form the basins of the Great Lakes. Thousands of years later the climate began to warm and the glaciers slowly retreated. The weight of the ice had pushed down the earth's crust and left large lakes bigger than the present ones. Many of the old lake shores can be seen above those of the present-day ones. Some of them are now gravel pits. When the weight of the ice was gone, the earth began to rise up toward its old level. The slow **rebound** (REE baund) changed the size of the lakes and the direction in which the rivers flowed. Plants began to grow and animals returned.

Three forms of transportation, river, road, and rail, make use of a deep glacial valley.

There were several ice ages like this over the next 8,000 years. We arrived at our present lakes and drainage system about 5,000 years ago. Since then, the lakes have not changed much, except for the effect human activity has had on them.

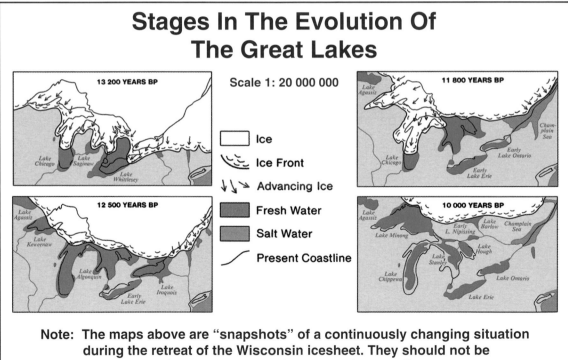

The stages of glaciation of the Lakes

The Route To The Fur Country

In the seventeenth century, the canoe trip along the length of the Great Lakes was extremely difficult. Tough French-Canadian paddlers called voyageurs (voy uh ZHUR) carried supplies along the waterways to the West and brought back the furs that the fur trappers had taken during the winter. Their diet of dried beans or peas, sea biscuits, and salt pork earned them the nickname of "bacon eaters."

They were mostly small men, small enough to fit into a canoe, but they were enormously strong. (They could paddle 14 to 16 hours a day and travel up to 75 miles). Their boats, called Montreal canoes, were 36 feet (11 meters) long and 6 feet (1.8 meters) wide, carried 3 tons (3,000 kilograms) of cargo, and had a crew of six to twelve paddlers. Though they had no metal in their construction, the canoes were strong enough to survive rapids on the rivers and rough waters on the lakes.

The voyageurs left Lachine, near Montreal, early in the year and paddled up the Ottawa River. Then they crossed to Lake Huron by way of Lake Nipissing and the French River. There were thirty-six **portages** (poor TAHZ iz) between Montreal and Lake Huron. At every one, the voyageurs carried at least two 90-pound (37 kilogram) bundles of trade goods at a time on their shoulders, and they even ran! They were in a hurry because the paddling season was short. Their route then followed the North Channel to Sault Sainte Marie, where they received extra food—corn shipped in from the southern lakes. From there, they followed the Saint Mary's River out onto the dangerous waters of Lake Superior, with still about 300 miles (480 kilometers) to paddle.

A voyageur with one of his 90-lb (37 kilogram) bundles

At the western end of Lake Ontario, the Welland Canal **bypasses** (BI pass iz) the Niagara River and carries ships into Lake Erie. The canal is 28 miles (45 kilometers) long and rises 326 feet (99.3 meters). After sailing west along Lake Erie, ships sail up the Detroit River, between Detroit, Michigan, and Windsor, Ontario, across Lake Saint Clair and then enter Lake Huron through the Saint Clair River. Huron is only 8 feet (2.5 meters) higher than Erie and no locks are needed.

At the northern end of Lake Huron, ships can follow two routes. They can pass through the Straits of Mackinac (MACK-i-naw), under the Mackinac Bridge, into Lake Michigan and go as far as Chicago. Lakes Huron and Michigan are at the same height above sea level. They can also follow the Saint Mary's River and pass through the Sault Sainte Marie locks into Lake Superior. The Saint Mary's River is 70 miles (112 kilometers) long, and ships must be lifted 24 feet (7.2 meters) in that distance. Duluth, the end of the journey, is at the western end of the lake. The deeper lakes do not freeze over completely, but shipping is closed down from mid-December to mid-April because ports and canals are frozen.

The locks at Sault Sainte Marie. The biggest can accommodate all ships.

The lakes connect with the Hudson River system through the New York State Barge Canal at Buffalo, Rochester, and Oswego, and to the Mississippi River through the Ohio Canal system at Chicago. The Rideau Canal connects eastern Lake Ontario to the Ottawa River.

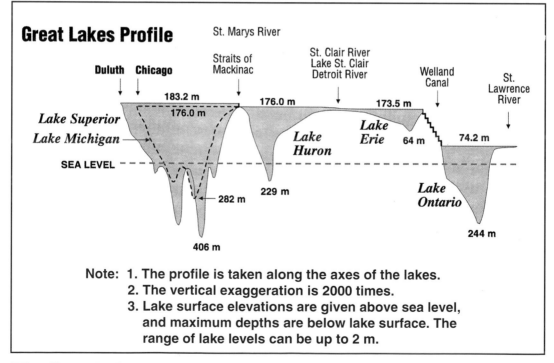

The Great Lakes Profile

THE WATER CYCLE AND THE CLIMATE

Water is a **flow resource** (FLO REE sors). It hangs in the air, it soaks into the ground, or it gathers as seas, lakes, or rivers. When water comes into contact with dry air, some of it **evaporates** (ee VAP uh rates) and becomes water vapor. The moisture may stay in the air as humidity, or it may cool to form clouds, fog, or mist.

This is important in the Great Lakes because they have large surface areas from which water can evaporate. Moisture also gets into the air from their forests, feeder lakes, and rivers.

Weather systems also bring their moisture over the lakes. Most of this moisture then falls as rain, sleet, hail, or snow on the lakes or on the surrounding land, and the cycle can begin again. In fact, the lakes can create their own climates.

In summer, warm, humid air sometimes flows up from the Gulf of Mexico, over the warm land and then over the cool lakes. As it passes over the water, the lower layer of air is cooled. This cooler, moist air stays trapped below the layer of warmer air above. When this happens, the southern regions of the lakes have some warm, humid days and nights, and occasional summer thunderstorms.

During the summer, the lake waters warm up. They warm up the cold winds of autumn and winter as they blow across the surface of the water. This helps to make these seasons a little milder.

In the late fall, cold air masses flowing down from the Arctic collide with warm air flowing in from the south. The mixing of the two air masses can create fierce storms. The November storm of 1913, which destroyed or damaged over 70 ships and killed nearly 250 sailors, is a famous example of such a storm.

Storm clouds gather over the lake.

Until the lakes freeze over in winter, very cold winds blow across the water, usually from the northwest, and pick up a lot of moisture. They then drop it as snow when they reach the southeast side of the lake. This is called lake effect snow.

Again in spring, warm and cold air masses clash and cause strong storms. Spring comes a little late because the lakes are still cold from the winter and they help to cool the land around them.

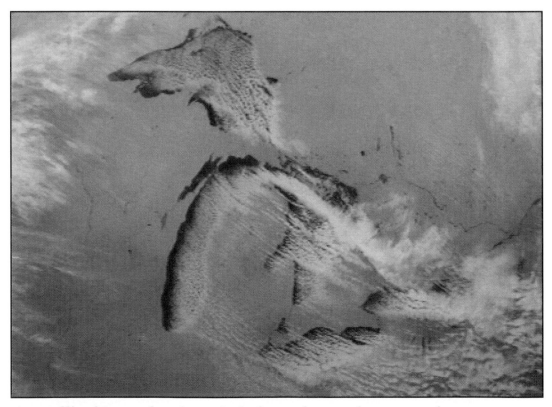

A satellite image showing winds from the northwest causing snow streamers

PROBLEMS FOR THE GREAT LAKES

The Great Lakes were clear and clean in the seventeenth century. Trapping and fishing for personal food did not affect them much. Pollution began to threaten the lakes as human activity increased. Fish habitat was destroyed when intensive logging caused erosion and runoff, and blocked and **diverted** (duh VURT id) streams. Agricultural fertilizers and animal wastes found their way into the lakes. Factories have been built on the lakes because of easy transportation links. They may allow outfall from their processes. They may also **emit** (ee MIT) pollutants into the atmosphere. These settle as dust or are absorbed by moisture and fall as acid rain or snow.

Cities have allowed untreated human waste and chemicals, such as street salt or phosphorus from detergents, to enter the lakes. Water soaking into the earth absorbs many chemicals from the soil and often ends up in the lakes. Because only one percent of the water leaves the lakes every year, pollutants stay in them a long time and may become quite concentrated. Wetlands that helped to control pollution have been drained in order to develop the land.

Nonnative fish have become a threat to the lakes. When the Welland Canal opened, sea lampreys were able to reach all the lakes. Zebra mussels probably arrived in the lakes in the ballast water of oceangoing ships. Now they clog intake pipes on anything from boat motors to power station cooling systems.

A wetland area

A European plant called purple loosestrife, which some people have cultivated for its beauty, is now recognized as a nuisance plant. It grows rapidly and replaces the native vegetation that is food and habitat for fish and wildlife.

Zebra mussels on the walls of a lock

REPAIRING THE DAMAGE

The first polluted beaches and **contaminated** (kun TAM uh nate id) water seemed to be local problems. However, by the 1960s, scientists were beginning to show that human activity was harming the ecosystem of all the lakes. The U.S. and Canadian governments began to make laws to control factory discharges and to help communities build good sewage treatment plants. Chemicals such as DDT that affect the whole food chain were banned. Cleanup steps and measures called Remedial Action Plans (RAPs) were prepared for geographic Areas of Concern (AOC).

The damming and diverting of streams and the development of sand dunes, wetlands and riverbanks were studied to see what effect these things might have on the ecosystem. The lakes are now much clearer. Restocking them with species of fish that were in danger of disappearing through overfishing or loss of habitat is becoming successful. Commercial fishing is limited to allow stocks to rebuild.

Lamprey are controlled in the river mud, where they hatch, by poison that affects only them and by barriers that keep adults out of streams, where they breed. Zebra mussels are still a problem, but scientists are working on it with some success. Beetles are being introduced to control purple loosestrife. Because the Great Lakes are so big, and so many different organizations are responsible for their health, people around them will have to watch and make sure that the problems that occurred in the past are not allowed to happen again.

Lamprey are parasitic fish which can eat 40 pounds (16 kilograms) of fish per year.

WORKING TOGETHER

Many organizations are working to preserve and improve the lakes. Every two years, the State of the Lakes Ecosystem Conferences, led by Environment Canada and the U.S. Environmental Protection Agency, issue reports on topics such as the health of wildlife and fish, the quality of the drinking water, and the state of the wetlands. The quality of the water is important to a city like Detroit, which takes the drinking water for 5 million people out of the Detroit River.

Young lake trout—called fry

The Great Lakes Commission at Ann Arbor, Michigan, represents eight states. It is developing a plan to manage the waters, land, and natural resources of the lakes.

The Sea Grant supports research and public education programs related to the Great Lakes. It offers summer teen camps, scholarship programs, classroom presentations, field trips, and video and print material. It also gives advice on fisheries, tourism, **aquaculture** (ah kwah KUL chur), and shipwreck preservation.

There are over forty "hot spots" on the lakes that need urgent attention, and the public must show interest and work to fix these problems. The Great Lakes 2000 Cleanup Fund (Environment Canada) supports community groups, universities, and interested citizens with information, technical advice, and financial aid. These are some of the groups that are working to make the lakes clean again, so that fish and wildlife habitats will improve and people will be able to enjoy these wonderful bodies of water in the future.

GLOSSARY

aquaculture (ah kwah KUL chur) — farming of water

bypass (BI pass) — go around, follow a detour

Canadian Shield (kuh NAY dee un SHE(u)LD) — a rocky area of low hills, forests and lakes. The rock lies under much of the Northeast

contaminated (kun TAM uh nate id) — made impure, polluted

divert (duh VURT) — change the direction of something that moves

emit (ee MIT) — send out

endurance (in DUR unts) — the ability to put up with

erode, erosion (eh RODE, eh RO zhun) — wear away, bit by bit

evaporate (ee VAP uh rate) — change from liquid into a gas

flow resource (FLO REE sors) — a resource that is constantly changing (running water, wind, etc.)

portage (poor TAHZ) — a stretch of land between water routes where goods and canoes must be carried

rebound (REE baund) — bounce back

INDEX

FURTHER READING

You can find out more about the Great Lakes with these helpful books and web sites:

- The Great Lakes-An Environmental Atlas and Resource Book, U.S.E.P.A. 77 West Jackson Boulevard, Chicago, IL, 60604
- Environment Canada, 4905 Dufferin St., Downsview, ON M3H 5T4
- Assoc. for Great Lakes Maritime History, P.O. Box 7365, Bowling Green, OH 43402

- Minnesota Sea Grant, University of Minnesota: www.d.umn.edu/seagr; seagr@d.umn.edu
- Michigan Sea Grant, University of Michigan: www.engin.umich.edu/seagrant
- The Great Lakes Commission: glc@great-lakes.net
- The Great Lakes Cleanup Fund (Environment Canada): John.Shaw@ec.gc.ca
- Great Lakes Information Management Resource (Environment Canada): www.cciw.ca/glimr
- Great Lakes Information Network: www.great-lakes.net/redesk/almanac/lakes
- Quizzes on the Lakes: www.hcbe.edu.on.ca/coll/lakes.htm